Written by Jean-Pierre Verdet
Illustrated by Christian Broutin, Henri Galeron and Pierre-Marie Valat

Specialist adviser: Dr Anita McConnell,
Curator, Earth Sciences Collection,
The Science Museum, London

ISBN 1 85103 020 4
First published 1987 in the United Kingdom by
Moonlight Publishing Ltd,
131 Kensington Church Street, London W8

© 1986 by Editions Gallimard
Translated by Sarah Matthews
English text © 1987 by Moonlight Publishing Ltd
Printed in Italy by La Editoriale Libraria

POCKET • WORLDS

The Sunshine Around Us

You can't hold it,
    you can't taste it,
        you can't do without it!

THE WORLD OF NATURE

Could you survive without the sun?
No!
You depend on it for heat and light. Even in prehistoric times, people realised its importance. Over four thousand years ago they built huge monuments to honour the sun.

The most famous of these monuments is **Stonehenge** in England. It is a circle of enormous stones standing on end. Next to the circle stands one stone on its own. This monument is not only a temple – it is an observatory too. If you were to stand in the middle of the circle at dawn on Midsummer Day, you could see the sun rising over the single standing stone!
It is a very beautiful sight.

Midsummer Day is the summer solstice and marks the beginning of the three hottest months of the year.

Since the beginning of time, men have told stories and legends about the sun.

For the **Sumerians,** who lived in Mesopotamia 5000 years ago, the sun was a god!

Every morning, scorpion-men opened the doors of his cave in the east. Then the sun-god climbed to the top of the mountain and set off across the sky in his chariot. The sun that we see was one of the wheels of that chariot. In the evening, the sun disappeared back into the mountain through its western door, and the scorpion-men shut the door behind him.

The sun was a god for the **Ancient Egyptians** as well. In fact, it was several gods! The luminous disc of the sun was the god Aton. The rising sun was the god Khepri. When it was at its highest point in the sky, it was Ra. And when it sank, it was Atum. It was also the god Horus sailing round the world on his boat. He travelled along constantly on the lookout for his eternal enemy, the flood serpent. Sometimes the serpent swallowed up Horus and his boat – that was a solar eclipse!

Other peoples believed the sun was an egg, freshly laid every morning by the Great Goose in the sky.

All life is due to the sun.

Plants use sunlight to combine carbon and other elements to grow new leaves.
Herbivorous animals eat the plants, and carnivorous animals eat the herbivores that have eaten the plants...
And we eat everything: plants, herbivores and carnivores. We eat sunshine!

The sun enables us to breathe; it is thanks to the sun that plants make the oxygen we need to live.

Trees, cereals, coal, oil, all come to us thanks to the sun.

The sun is the source of almost all the energy in the world!

Every year the sun helps millions of tonnes of timber to grow, to make fires to warm us. Decaying trees and plants in the end become natural gas, coal and oil.

Sun-traps

When the sun's rays pass through the glass panes of a greenhouse, it is as if the sun has been trapped; it is much hotter inside the greenhouse than outside. The plants inside grow faster! Photo-electric cells make it possible to turn solar energy directly into electricity.

In Africa, electricity produced by photo-electric cells pumps water from wells.

Heat from the sun draws up water from rivers and seas. The water, falling as rain, fills rivers and lakes.

The only energy which does not come from the sun is the nuclear energy that is generated in atomic power-stations.

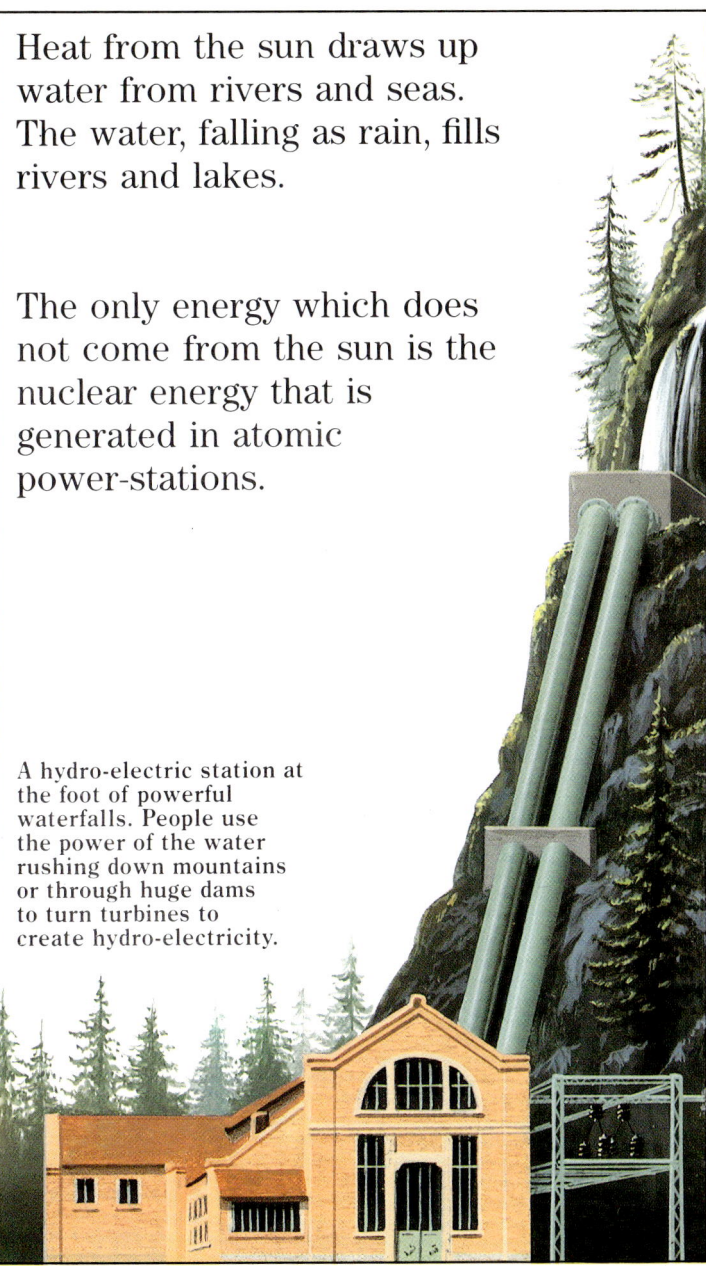

A hydro-electric station at the foot of powerful waterfalls. People use the power of the water rushing down mountains or through huge dams to turn turbines to create hydro-electricity.

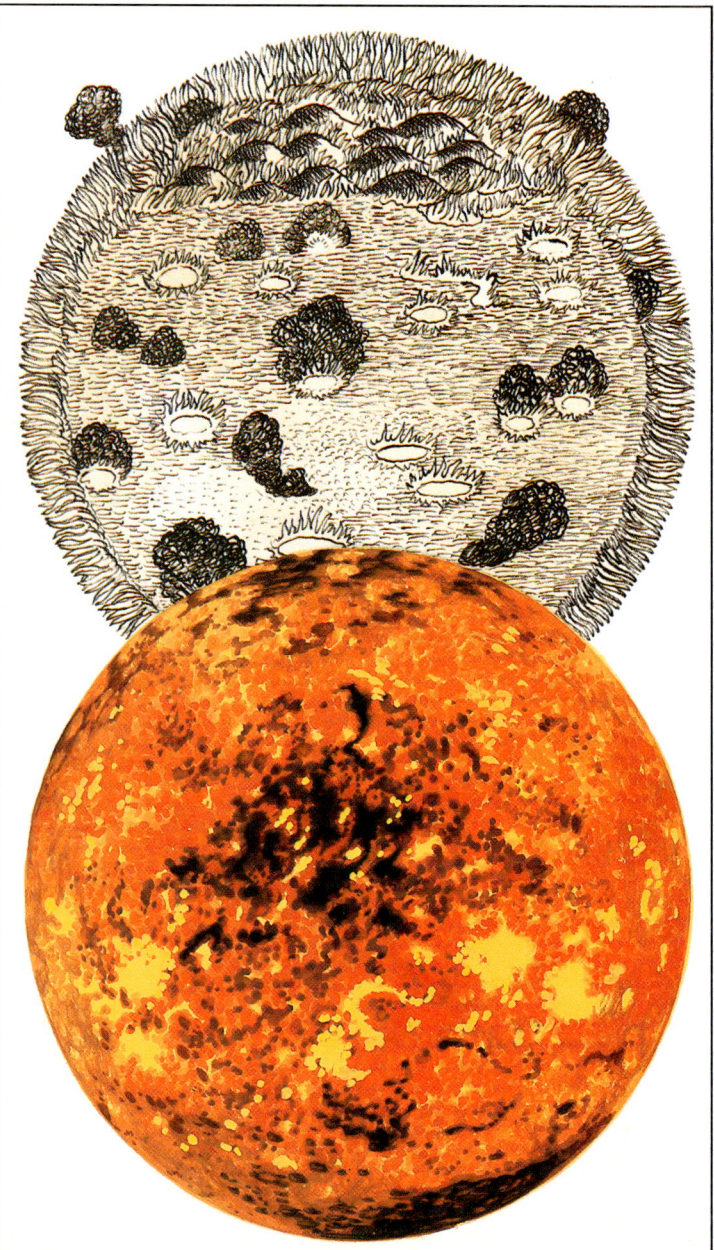

The sun is not a ball of fire.
If it were a very big lump of burning coal, it would only have lasted for 7000 years. But it's been shining for a lot longer than that!
The sun is a star, a ball of very hot gases: it is several million degrees centigrade at the centre of the sun. The centre is a huge hydrogen bomb, but a stable bomb which has been exploding gently for over 5 billion years, and which will go on exploding for as long again. The sun is halfway through its life! Look at this picture of the sun as it was thought to be in the 17th century, and as it can be seen in the picture underneath today reflected through a telescope (never study the sun directly – it can damage your eyes).

Sometimes matter shoots up from the sun's surface and falls back again: this is a solar eruption.

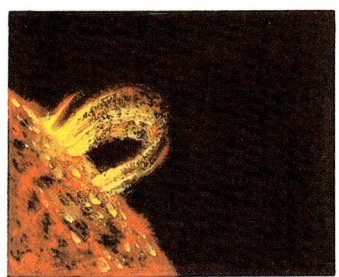 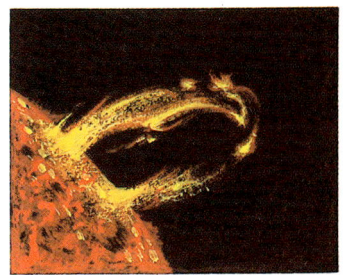

Every day, the sun seems to travel in a huge arch right across the sky!

In the morning, it rises in the east and climbs the sky, until it is high in the south at midday. In the evening it sinks in the west and night falls.

You are looking south. The sun rises in the east.

At midday it is at its highest point: the zenith.
See how the shadows change.

All the same, the sun does not move. It is the Earth which turns right round once every 24 hours.

It sinks in the west.

At midday, the valley is filled with light.

The shadows lengthen as the sun sinks.

The Earth revolves around the sun.

We feel very still and stable on our planet, as if the Earth stood quite still in the middle of the sky, as for a very long time people believed it did.
In fact, though, the Earth sweeps round the sun in an enormous journey of almost a billion kilometres – it takes a whole year to do it!

That journey gives us the four seasons. But the Earth is not closer to the sun in summer. It is because the sun's rays fall straight onto the Earth, and not at an angle, and because the days are longer in summer, that it is hotter then.

It is **winter**: the nights are longer than the days. It grows dark before five o'clock in the afternoon.
In **spring,** the days and nights are the same length.

The sun is low in the sky, it is cold.

Day by day the sun climbs a little higher.

The days are longer, it is lighter in the evenings; it is **summer.** But the **autumn** is soon here; once more day and night are the same length.

The sun is at its highest point in the sky.

The sun is closer to the horizon.

In western Europe, the length of the days and nights varies by several hours during the year. Near the equator, there are twelve hours of daylight and twelve hours of the night all year long.

The midnight sun
But at the Poles, the day lasts for six months, and then there comes a night six months long! During the summer, the sun seems to move across the sky without ever setting.

At midnight, it gets close to the horizon, then rises again without ever having gone out of sight...

The **Polar auroras** are a wonderful sight for people in the far north and south... Green, gold and purple, they light up the sky in huge curtains of colour. You can see one on the next page!

People in Europe live half-way between the North Pole and the equator; the sun never passes directly overhead. But near the equator, at midday, the sun is straight above you. Shadows are at their shortest and light falls to the bottom of even the deepest well!

The Earth is not alone in its journey round the sun.

Eight other planets travel along with it; Mercury (1), Venus (2), Mars (3), Jupiter (4), Saturn (5), Uranus (6), Neptune (7), and Pluto (8). The Earth is tucked between Venus and Mars.

There are also comets, which come from great distances beyond the solar system, and meteors tumbling like stones through space.

The relative sizes of the planets

Between Mars and Jupiter, you can see a whole lot of little planets; astronomers think they are left over from a big planet which exploded.

Why does the moon sometimes hide the sun? After all, it is much smaller than the sun! But it is also much closer to the Earth, and so to us the sun and the moon look about the same size. While the Earth takes a year to go around the sun, the moon takes a month to circle the Earth. About once every year, it passes between the Earth and the sun, and blots out part or all of the sun's disc for a few minutes.

Sun

Moon

Earth

This is a solar eclipse!

Only the people living between the lines joining the moon and the sun on the picture can actually see the eclipse: you can't see one every year... unless you travel a lot!

During an eclipse, hens think it is night-time and go back to bed!

Some animals, like bats, love the dark. But most animals, and people, and plants, prefer the sunshine. But **be careful: don't stare at the sun, or lie out in it too long** – you can get badly burnt!

White reflects the sun's rays; if you wear white you don't get so hot. That's why, in hot countries, houses and clothes are often white – it keeps the people cooler. **Black absorbs heat;** if you wear black, you will get hotter, but you will cool down more quickly in the shade.

Moles live underground and hate sunlight.

If you watch your shadow on a sunny day, you will see that it moves during the day and gets shorter and longer. Every day, at mid day, it will point north-south. That is also the time of day when your shadow is at its shortest because the sun is at its highest point overhead.

If you mark the position of your shadow every hour during the day, you can make yourself a sundial.

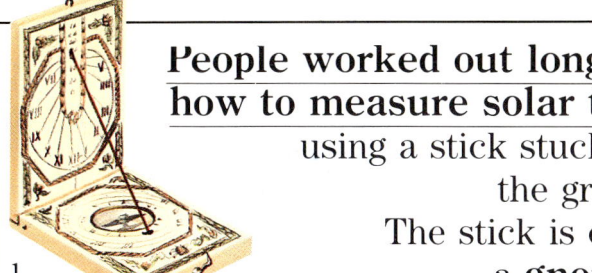

People worked out long ago how to measure solar time,

using a stick stuck into the ground. The stick is called a **gnomon**.

Then they used the gnomon in more complicated instruments, and made **sundials.** Some of these were no bigger than an alarm clock; people could take one with them on journeys (1)!

The outside walls of churches and houses, whether big or small, were often decorated with sundials (2).

Some garden sundials were real works of art (3)!

The Mayas in Central America, the Aztecs in Mexico and the Incas in Peru worshipped the sun. They built temples in the shape of pyramids so huge they have astonished later generations.

Index

Earth, 20-21, 28-29
eclipses, 31
energy, 12-13
heat, 7, 32
legends, 8-9
life, 11
light, 7, 32
movement, 16-17, 20-21
planets, 28-29
seasons, 21-25
shadows, 27, 34
star, 15
sundials, 34-35
sun-traps, 12